CW00345343

THE
BARTENDER'S
GUIDE TO
RUM

THE BARTENDER'S GUIDE TO

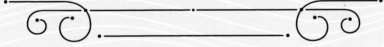

RUM

CLASSIC AND MODERN-DAY COCKTAILS FOR RUM LOVERS

LOVE FOOD™

HISTORY OF RUM

The evolution of rum has been shaped by various historical events spanning many centuries – from purely medicinal use, dark years of slavery and pirates, to the rum cocktails we know today crafted by modern mixologists. One element remains at the heart of the story – sugar – but what other factors came into play in rum's spirited history?

Rum, like all distilled spirits, shares a common ancestor in the first stills that were filled by Arabic alchemists as early as the 1st century. This was when the Roman Empire was in full swing and Christianity appeared. These early scientists spent decades distilling all manner of elixirs, gleaning knowledge from the Greeks, amongst other sources.

By the 12th century, the knowledge had spread further across Europe and was being nurtured in the hands of Benedictine monks in Salerno, Italy. At this point, spirit was utilized purely for

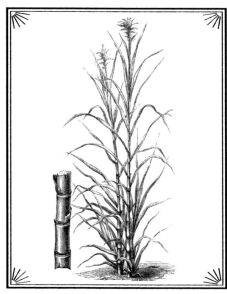

medicinal and scientific reasons, being used to preserve rare and precious ingredients used in medicine. From Italy, the science of distillation began to grow through the monasteries, right across Europe and the known world. The process was still crude, but over the centuries it was continuously improved by Europe's scientific minds. By the 17th century, distillation was in full swing and we began to see the commercialization of distilled spirits.

Of all the commodities of the ancient and modern world, sugar is undoubtedly amongst the most significant, shaping empires and the very trade routes and shipping lanes that are still used today. The importance of sugar cultivation in the ancient world right through into the 21st century cannot be understated. Where sugar has been cultivated, rum production has nearly always followed.

The precise origins of the very first distilled spirits derived from sugar cane are uncertain, but the birth of rum as we know it can find its roots in the sugar-cane plantations of the Caribbean, cultivated by the Portuguese, Dutch, French and English empires as early as the 16th century.
Throughout the 16th century, Europe was developing an incredibly sweet tooth and a fondness for sweetness that is still very much alive today. The climate and soils in the Caribbean suited sugar cane perfectly and, with very small indigenous populations, the islands and their population were subjected to exploitation by these larger empires. For the next two centuries, the colonial plantations of the Caribbean, as well as plantations in South America, would provide 90 per cent of the growing demand for sugar from Europe.

It was Christopher Columbus who first introduced sugar cane to the Caribbean on his 2nd voyage to the Americas in 1493. One of the consequences of the creation of links between Europe, the Caribbean and the Americas was the African slave trade – one of the largest movements of people the world has seen.

The trade triangle between Europe, the Caribbean and the America was formed, where sugar, molasses and rum were shipped from the Caribbean into Europe and the Americas. Rum and European goods were then shipped to Africa and traded for African people, who were in turn sold as slaves and sent to the Caribbean and the Americas to work on plantations. It's estimated that over 11 million Africans were taken on ships heading to the Americas to work on plantations between the 16th and 19th centuries.

With so much rum being shipped around the world at this time, rum and molasses

started to be used as currency and became synonymous with the Royal Navy and as a drink of privateers. During the 1700s, the power and influence of the sugar trade was growing, reaching into the UK parliament with powerful lobbyists championing rum as a noble and exotic alternative to spirits such as gin and brandy, both of which were suffering major reputational damage due to associations with war and poverty.

It was rum's time to shine and with a solid supply of molasses and spirit from the colonies, rums that were produced in the Caribbean, New England (US), Bristol and London began to flow into the glasses of England's aristocracy and middle classes, normally in the form of a spiced punch. With the abolition of slavery during the 1800s, the production of Caribbean sugar fell and so did the molasses that was being used to make rum. The French responded by producing large volumes of sugar domestically from beets and for the first time rum began to rival sugar in value as an article of trade. Throughout the 1800s, major advances in distillation and a better understanding of barrel ageing emerged and the quality of rum as a whole improved dramatically.

In the first half of the 20th century, the Scottish and Irish whisky industries were

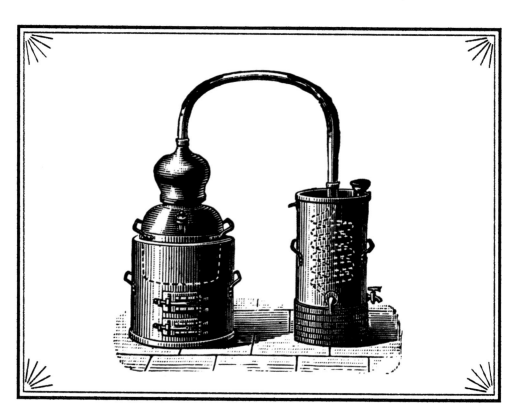

slowing down. They were starved of the grains they needed to produce whisky due to the two World Wars. With molasses being a by-product of the sugar industry and having no use as a foodstuff, the production of rum continued. Rum producers seized the opportunity to fill the empty glasses, quenching the thirst for strong spirits. With the rise of Tiki bars and cocktails, the popularity of rum was rising and moving away from its dark past and associations with slavery.

In the 1960s the West Indies Rum & Spirits Producers' Association (WIRSPA) was set up to help promote and protect the interests of its member distilleries and help in the marketing and export of Caribbean rum worldwide. More recently WIRSPA set up the Authentic

Caribbean Rum marque (ACR) with the goal to create a visual symbol to help the identification of genuine Caribbean rums.

In more recent years, rums of very high quality are being produced by distillers all over the world, but Caribbean rum in particular has started to gain international recognition by spirit experts. Nearly 400 years since the first rums were produced in the Caribbean, rum is finally taking its rightful place as one of the world's finest spirits alongside prestigious whiskies and Cognacs. A mighty journey and eventful history that can be found in every glass of rum, no matter where it's from.

PRODUCTION OF RUM

All complex, flavourful spirits can boast a varied and diverse production process, but none more so than rum. Being made the world over, the production of rum (or sugar cane based spirits), and the techniques used in distillation, are almost infinite. To best understand rum you first need to have an understanding of how alcohol is made.

All alcoholic drinks are the product of a serendipitous relationship between yeast and sugar. Yeast is a single celled organism and a fungus which within the right conditions can transform the fermentable sugars in a sugary liquid into alcohol. The origin of the base liquid will determine the type of beverage being made. In the case of rum the base liquid is either made from molasses or pure sugar cane juice. The art of fermentation has been manipulated by man for thousands of years and evolved into different alcoholic beverages we see today. A fortuitous relationship that has been at the heart of many civilizations and cultures, both ancient and modern.

In its simplest form rum is produced by fermenting molasses or pure sugar cane juice to make an alcoholic solution known as wash. This can then be taken forward to distillation in either pot or column stills, or both. Following distillation some producers will then mature their rums in oak casks, further mellowing the spirit with complex flavours found in oak. Most rums start life as molasses which is a by-product of sugar cane. Sugar cane is harvested and pressed to release the cane juice. The juice is then boiled on a series of pots reducing the solution to a syrup. After the final boiling stage the remaining syrupy liquid is left to cool, it's at this point sugar crystals will begin to form, leaving behind a thick dark liquid known as molasses.

The molasses is then usually diluted with water and then fermented to create an alcoholic solution known as wash. This step in production can vary enormously between producers. Different yeast strains and fermentation times can have a big impact in forming different flavours. After fermentation a wash of around 8% ABV will be taken forward to be distilled. The types of still used varies from distillery to distillery. With each still capable of creating a unique distillate the door is kicked open to almost limitless variations.

Pot stills help create a richer and more flavourful spirit, whereas column stills will strip out more impurities in the spirt creating a lighter style. In some cases stills involving both pots and columns will be used.

During distillation the distiller will isolate the sweet spot in the spirit run known as the middle cut or heart of the run. This will then be taken forward to maturation or bottling. In the case of white rums it's usually straight to the bottling plant with your spirit. But if maturation is on the cards then the process is much more interesting.

Oak casks which have previously held Bourbon or Sherry are typically used. But where maturation can vary enormously is in the climate where the casks will rest. The immense heat in the Caribbean can create a rapid maturation effect as the spirit expands and is forced into the pores of the oak. As it cools and the spirit retracts, it brings with it lactones and flavour compounds from the cask, which not only bring a deep and interesting flavour but also colour.

The down side to the intense heat is the evaporation of the spirt from the casks, known as the angels share. In some rum distilleries as much as 10% a year can be lost to evaporation. To try and slow this down some producers will mature their rums in cooler warehouses. In some extreme cases they might even move casks up mountains or underground.

In a perfect world all aged rums would be natural colour, but this is rarely the case. Prior to bottling many rum producers will sweeten their rum in a similar way to Cognac producers. Regulations on how much sugar can be added back into the rum prior to bottling vary, but in many cases permitted amounts sit around 5%. This might not sound like a lot but can have a big impact on the final spirit in the bottle and not always in a good way.

Ahead of bottling, vatting has to be considered. If the producer has several still types and a large inventory of aged stocks, casks of various ages and spirit types will be combined. This is done to create a uniform style and help achieve consistency from batch to batch. Ensuring in principle that every time you pick up a bottle of that expression it should taste the same.

Where rum excels in production is in the use of combined and hybrid stills. Their production process can be fantastically complex, requiring master distillers with immense skill and attention to detail.

TYPES OF RUM

With an almost infinite number of production twists and cultural turns, the idea of what rum is and how it's made can vary enormously. Unlike most other spirits rum remains undefined by a complete set of industry definitions. Production methods considered normal practice in one country or distillery may be considered sacrilege in another. But where some may see rum as an undefinable giant of the spirits industry others see an untameable charm.

GENERAL GLOBAL CATEGORIES

White Rums

Nearly always un-aged and often deemed inferior to dark/aged rums, white rums are the usual choice for most backbars and often seen as vodka's slightly better-looking sister. However, some fantastic white rums can be found and in some cases producers will actually take aged spirit through a charcoal filtration process to remove the colour, producing white rums with greater depth of flavour.

Dark Rums

Drawing their colour from barrel ageing and usually based on molasses as opposed to pure cane juice, the dark rum category is vast. It encompasses rums of high quality to the bottom-shelf varieties. Sometimes the cheaper varieties will be un-aged spirit darkened with caramel and sweetened prior to bottling. This might be done to give the illusion of ageing in casks.

Navy Rums

A blend of dark rums, typically built around rums from Guyana and usually originating from distilleries found in the British West Indies. Navy Rum became synonymous with dark rum and vice versa during its rise in popularity with the Royal Navy in the 19th century. Navy strength rums would fall into the overproof bracket below.

Overproof Rums

In the EU the minimum strength for bottling rum is 37.5% ABV whereas in the US the minimum is 40% ABV. The term 'overproof' refers to rums with a higher than usual bottling strength and typically fall around 50–70% ABV. Before the use of hydrometers alcohol strength in spirits was simply measured by using gunpowder in what was known as the gunpowder test. A small amount of gunpowder would be soaked in the spirit, a spark of flame would then be put to the powder. If it ignited the spirit would be proven and therefore considered overproof. In short, overproof in modern terms, means wickedly strong.

Spiced Rums

The quality and quantity of additives used to sweeten and flavour spiced rums varies enormously between the different varieties. Mainstream and cheaper spiced rums are usually flavoured and coloured heavily using sugar, spices and caramel. In extreme cases some are so heavily laced with flavourings, that they can't technically qualify as rum in some markets. Despite leaning more towards a liqueur than a true rum, the 'spiced' style has become hugely popular when served with mixers, like coke or ginger beer.

RUM, BUT NOT RUM

Rhum Agricole

Originating from the island of Martinique and the French West Indies, this style of rum takes its cues from the French colonials and can only be made from domestic cane crops and the resulting pure cane juice. Rhum Agricole is the only cane derived spirit to carry an Appellation d'Origine Contrôlée mark (AOC), a mark usually reserved for French wine producers. Some of the finest distillates on the planet can be found in this category.

Cachaça

Brazil's answer to rum, and taking its name from the Dutch word for sugarcane. Cachaça is made from only pure cane juice and is, in principal, similar to the Agricole style of the French West Indies. However production differences surrounding alcohol strength, origins of their cane and distillation strengths mean they are in fact quite different. Some of the planets biggest distilleries are making cachaça but finding truly great examples of this spirit outside of Brazil can be tricky.

Indian Rum and the Far East

Various countries are producing vast amounts of sugar and therefore molasses. This is fermented and made into spirit, again of various styles using pot and column stills in distilleries big and small. In many cases these distillates are destined to be sold domestically, and to make things really confusing are sometimes blended with small amounts of grain-based spirit and often labelled as whisky. Some producers do label as rum however and are fantastic to drink.

GLASSWARE

It is important to serve a cocktail in the appropriate glass – the size, shape and style all have an impact on the visual perception and enjoyment of the drink. Here are some of the classic glasses that you will need to have in your collection.

Martini glass

The most iconic of all cocktail glasses, the conical martini glass emerged with the art deco movement. The long stem is perfect for chilled drinks as it keeps people's hands from inadvertently warming the cocktail.

Highball glass

Sometimes also known as a Collins glass, these glasses are perfect for serving drinks with a high proportion of mixer to spirit.

Lowball glass

The lowball glass, also known as a rocks or old-fashioned glass, is a short, squat tumbler and is great for serving any spirit on the rocks or for short, mixed cocktails.

Champagne flute

The tall, thin flute's tapered design reduces the Champagne's surface area and so helps to keep the fizz in the drink for longer.

Shot glass

This glass is a home-bar essential and can hold just enough spirit to be drunk in one mouthful. The shot glass can also stand in for a measure when making cocktails.

Coupette glass

Legend has it that the coupette or Margarita glass is modelled on a woman's breast. The coupette is now used to serve Margaritas and Daiquiris.

Coupe glass

Another wide-rimmed glass that is good for serving sparkling drinks. The short-stemmed coupe is also used for serving Daiquiris.

Snifter glass

The bowl-shaped snifter glass invites the drinker to cradle the drink in their hands, warming the contents of the glass. The aroma of the drink is held in the glass, allowing you to breathe in the drink before sipping.

Hurricane glass

This pear-shaped glass pays homage to the hurricane lamp and was the glass used to create the New Orleans rum-based cocktail, Hurricane. It's also used for a variety of frozen and blended cocktails.

Sling glass

A variation on the highball glass, this is a design classic that is used to serve Long Island Ice Tea and the Mojito. Its tall body and short stem make it ideal for chilled drinks.

MIXOLOGY KIT

What equipment you have in your home bar depends on whether you like all the latest gadgets, or whether you are prepared to make do with some basic options. Nowadays, there is no limit to the amount of bar equipment available, but you don't need lots of kit to make most of the drinks in this book. Here are some of the essential tools of the trade that you'll need.

Measures and jiggers

A jigger is a bartender's basic measuring tool and essential for crafting the perfect blend of ingredients. Get a steel jigger with clear measurement markings so you can easily and accurately pour out measures.

Bar spoon

A proper bar spoon has a small bowl and a long handle that allows you to muddle, mix and stir with ease. Spoons come in a variety of lengths and widths and a stylishly designed bar spoon is an attractive addition to any bartender's kit.

Shaker

Most contemporary shakers are made from steel as they don't tarnish easily and they don't conduct heat easily – this is useful with chilled cocktails as the ice cools the cocktail rather than the shaker. Most standard shakers come with a built-in strainer, but if you're using a Boston or Parisian shaker then you'll need to use a separate strainer.

Mixing glass or beaker

Any vessel that holds about 500 ml/1 pint of liquid can be used for mixing drinks. It is good to have a mixing glass with a spout so that you can stop ice from slipping into the glass. Mixing beakers are increasingly popular and are usually made of glass or crystal.

Muddler

For mashing up citrus fruit or crushing herbs, you need a muddler. This is a chunky wooden tool with a rounded end and it can also be used to make cracked ice.

Strainer

A bar or Hawthorne strainer is an essential tool to prevent ice and other ingredients being poured into your glass. Some cocktails need to be double strained so even if there is a strainer in your cocktail shaker, you'll still need a separate Hawthorne strainer.

Juicer

A traditional, ridged half-lemon shape on a saucer will work perfectly well for juicing small amounts. There is also a citrus spout that screws into a lemon or lime and is useful for obtaining tiny amounts of juice.

Other equipment

Other items you might need in your home-bar equipment are: corkscrew, bottle opener, cocktail sticks, blender, tongs, ice bucket, chopping board, knives, jugs, swizzle sticks, and straws.

TECHNIQUES

Shaking and Stirring

These are the two most basic mixology techniques, but they are essential to master in order to make any cocktail with confidence.

Shaking is when you add all of the ingredients, with the specified amount of ice cubes, to the shaker and then shake vigorously for approximately 5–10 seconds. The benefits of shaking are that the drink is rapidly mixed, chilled and aerated. Once the drink has been shaken, the outside of the shaker should be lightly frosted.

Shaking a cocktail also dilutes the drink quite significantly. This dilution is an essential as it gives the correct balance of taste, strength and temperature. The drink is then double strained into glasses – the shaker should have an inbuilt strainer and

you usually use a separate strainer over the glass as well. Shaking can also be used to prepare cocktails that include an ingredient, such as an egg white, that will not combine with less vigorous forms of mixing.

Stirring is the purist's choice – it's where you add all the ingredients, usually with some ice cubes, but this time you combine them in a mixing glass or beaker and then stir the ingredients together using a bar spoon or swizzle stick. As with shaking, this allows you to blend and chill the ingredients without too much erosion of the ice, so you can control the level of dilution and keep it to a minimum.

Building and Layering

Building is a mixology technique, a technical term for the task of pouring all the ingredients, one by one, usually over ice, into the glass in which the cocktail will be served. You might then stir the cocktail briefly, but this is just to mix rather than for chilling or aerating. It is important to follow built recipes exactly as the order of the ingredients can change from drink to drink and this can affect the final flavour.

Another important skill that the bartender must acquire is the art of layering, which requires greater precision and a steadier hand. To make layered shooters or other drinks, you generally pour the heaviest liquid first, working through to the lightest. However, the real trick is the technique. Either touch the top of the drink with a long-handled bar spoon and pour the liquid slowly over the back of it to disperse it across the top of the ingredients already in the glass, or pour the liquid down the twisted stem that many bar spoons have. You should hold the spoon's flat disc just above the drink. Be sure to use a clean bar spoon for each layer. Floating is the term used to describe adding the top layer.

Muddling and Blending

Muddling is the term used to describe the extraction of the juice or oils from the pulp or skin of a fruit, herb or spice. It involves mashing ingredients to release their flavours and it's usually done with a muddler.

As the name suggests, blending is when all the ingredients are combined in a blender. This technique is often used when mixing alcohol with fruit or with creamy ingredients that do not combine well unless they are blended. These drinks are often blended with crushed or cracked ice to produce cocktails with a smooth, frozen consistency. Popular blended drinks are Frozen Daiquiris and Coladas.

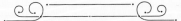

CHAPTER 1

CLASSIC CONCOCTIONS

The classics can be relied on time and time again. Steeped in history, tried and tested by rum lovers across the world, these are the staple players on the cocktail menu. Here you'll find the favourites, like the Rum Cooler, Mojito, Piña Colada and Hurricane. They combine traditional flavours and techniques, perfected by bartenders over the years and many form the basis of some of the new twists we see in modern cocktail bars today.

MOJITO

SERVES 1
INGREDIENTS

1 tsp sugar syrup

few mint leaves, plus extra
to decorate

juice of ½ lime, plus lime
slice to decorate

ice cubes

2 measures Jamaican rum

soda water

dash Angostura bitters

1. Put the syrup, mint leaves and lime juice in a chilled cocktail glass and crush or muddle the mint leaves.

2. Add ice and the rum, then top up with soda water to taste.

3. Finish with a dash of Angostura bitters and decorate with the mint leaves and lime slice. Serve immediately.

PIÑA COLADA

SERVES 1

INGREDIENTS

crushed ice

2 measures white rum

1 measure dark rum

3 measures
pineapple juice

2 measures
coconut cream

pineapple wedges,
to decorate

1. Put the crushed ice in a blender with the white rum, dark rum, pineapple juice and coconut cream and blend until smooth.

2. Strain, without stirring, into a chilled cocktail glass and decorate with pineapple wedges. Serve immediately.

DAIQUIRI

SERVES 1

INGREDIENTS

2 measures white rum

¼ measure lime juice

½ tsp sugar syrup

cracked ice

lime wedge, to decorate

1. Shake the rum, lime juice and sugar syrup over cracked ice until well frosted.

2. Strain into a chilled cocktail glass filled with ice. Decorate with a lime wedge. Serve immediately.

DARK & STORMY

SERVES 1

INGREDIENTS

2 measures golden rum

1 measure lime juice

½ measure sugar syrup

cracked ice

ginger beer

lime slice, to decorate

1. Shake the golden rum, lime juice and sugar syrup over cracked ice until well frosted. Strain into a chilled cocktail glass filled with ice and top up with ginger beer to taste.

2. Decorate with a lime slice. Serve immediately.

HURRICANE

SERVES 1

INGREDIENTS

4 measures dark rum

1 measure lemon juice

2 measures orange and passion fruit juice

cracked ice

soda water

orange slices and cocktail cherries, to decorate

1. Shake the dark rum, lemon juice and orange and passion fruit juice over cracked ice until well frosted.

2. Strain into a chilled cocktail glass filled with ice and top up with soda water.

3. Decorate with the orange slices and cherries. Serve immediately.

EL PRESIDENTE

SERVES 1

INGREDIENTS

2 measures white rum

1 measure dry vermouth

1 measure dry curaçao

dash grenadine

cracked ice

1 maraschino cherry and orange peel, to decorate

1. Shake the white rum, vermouth and curaçao with a dash of grenadine over cracked ice until well frosted.

2. Strain into a chilled cocktail glass, add a cherry to the base and decorate the top of the glass with orange peel. Serve immediately.

HISTORY OF THE MOJITO

The most famous rum cocktail that's available in almost every cocktail bar – the mojito's simple combination of white rum, mint, lime and soda makes a refreshing hit in warmer climes.

The classic mojito can trace its origins all the way back to the early 16th century when a drink began to emerge in Cuba called the Draque. This was a drink carved into history by none other than Sir Francis Drake, the famous privateer charged by Queen Elizabeth I to raid Spanish ships and cities in the emerging colonies.

It was upon Drake's arrival to Cuba in the 1580s that the drink is first referenced. Drake's ship was anchored offshore and the cities inhabitants watched and waited for what they thought was an inevitable attack. However, Drake's crew were suffering from numerous illnesses and it's believed that a small party of the men went ashore to Havana and collected the classic Mojito ingredients as medicine. To the relief of the city and its officials, the attack never came and Drake sailed away. How the drink took its name from the event is uncertain, but what is known is that the drink using cane spirit, water, mint and sugar was being consumed for medicinal reasons.

RUM COOLER

SERVES 1

INGREDIENTS

cracked ice

1½ measures white rum

1½ measures pineapple juice

1 banana, peeled and sliced

juice of 1 lime

lime peel twist, to decorate

1. Put cracked ice, the white rum, pineapple juice and banana into a blender. Add the lime juice and blend until smooth.

2. Strain into a chilled cocktail glass filled with ice.

3. Decorate with lime peel. Serve immediately.

CLASSIC RUM PUNCH

SERVES 1

INGREDIENTS

1 measure fresh lime juice

1½ measures sugar syrup

2 measures golden rum

cracked ice

lime curls, to decorate

1. Shake the lime juice, sugar syrup and golden rum over cracked ice until well frosted.

2. Strain into a chilled cocktail glass filled with ice. Decorate with a long lime curl. Serve immediately.

THE
RUM RANCH

SERVES 1
INGREDIENTS

1 slice deseeded red chilli, plus extra piece to decorate

2 measures golden rum

2 tsp sugar syrup

2 tsp fresh lemon juice

2 tsp fresh orange juice

dash Angostura bitters or Pimento bitters

cracked ice

orange and lemon slices, to decorate

1. Add the red chilli to the base of a cocktail shaker and muddle, or use the end of a rolling pin, to release the flavour.

2. Add the golden rum, sugar syrup and fruit juices to the shaker with a few drops of Angostura bitters and a handful of cracked ice. Shake vigorously until well frosted, then strain into a chilled cocktail glass filled with ice.

3. Decorate with orange and lemon slices and a piece of red chilli. Serve immediately.

MAE NAM

SERVES 1

INGREDIENTS

2 measures golden rum

2 tbsp fresh lime juice

1 tbsp Aromatic Sugar Syrup (see below)

cracked ice

1 lemon grass stem, trimmed and halved lengthways, to decorate

AROMATIC SUGAR SYRUP

115 g/4 oz palm or light muscovado sugar

125 ml/4 fl oz water

10-cm/4-inch piece lemon grass, halved lengthways

1-cm/½-inch piece fresh ginger, peeled and sliced

red chilli

1. To make the aromatic sugar syrup, add the sugar and water to a small saucepan then add the lemon grass, ginger and chilli. Heat gently, stirring occasionally until the sugar has dissolved then boil for 1 minute. Leave to cool for at least 1 hour for the flavours to infuse, then strain the mixture through a muslin. Pour into a sterilized, sealable jar.

2. To make the cocktail, shake the golden rum, lime juice and a tablespoon of the Aromatic Sugar Syrup over cracked ice until well frosted. The rest of the syrup can be stored in the refrigerator for up to a week.

3. Strain into a chilled cocktail glass filled with ice. Decorate with the lemon grass. Serve immediately.

LONG ISLAND ICED TEA

SERVES 1

INGREDIENTS

1 measure vodka

1 measure gin

1 measure white tequila

1 measure white rum

½ measure white crème de menthe

2 measures lemon juice

cracked ice

1 tsp caster sugar

cola

lime wedge, to decorate

1. Shake the vodka, gin, tequila, white rum, white crème de menthe and lemon juice over cracked ice until well frosted. Add the sugar and shake vigorously.

2. Strain into a chilled cocktail glass filled with ice.

3. Top up with cola, decorate with a lime wedge. Serve immediately.

JAMAICAN MULE

SERVES 1
INGREDIENTS

2 measures Jamaican rum

cracked ice

ginger beer

squeeze of lime juice

lime slice, to decorate

1. Pour the Jamaican rum into a chilled cocktail glass filled with ice.

2. Top up with ginger beer, add a squeeze of lime and decorate with a lime slice. Serve immediately.

MELLOW MULE

SERVES 2

INGREDIENTS

2 measures white rum

1 measure dark rum

1 measure golden rum

1 measure falernum (sweet ginger syrup)

1 measure lime juice

cracked ice

ginger beer

fruit slices, to decorate

1. Shake the white rum, dark rum, golden rum, falernum and lime juice over cracked ice until well frosted.

2. Strain into chilled cocktail glasses.

3. Top up with ginger beer and decorate with fruit slices. Serve immediately.

HOT BUTTERED RUM

SERVES 1

INGREDIENTS

1 measure dark rum

1 tsp soft dark brown sugar

150 ml/5 fl oz hot water

1 tsp salted butter

¼ tsp allspice

1. In a lowball glass, mix together the rum, brown sugar and hot water with a teaspoon until the sugar has completely dissolved.

2. Place the butter on top. Sprinkle over the allspice.

3. Serve immediately, when the butter has melted.

MAI TAI

SERVES 1

INGREDIENTS

1 measure white rum

1 measure dark rum

1 measure orange curaçao

1 measure lime juice

1 tbsp orgeat syrup

1 tbsp grenadine

cracked ice

fruit slices, to decorate

1. Shake the white and dark rums, curaçao, lime juice, orgeat and grenadine vigorously over cracked ice until well frosted.

2. Strain into a chilled cocktail glass and decorate with fruit slices. Serve immediately.

CLASSIC CONCOCTIONS

CHAPTER 2

SIMPLE
NOTES

Sometimes simplicity is best.
Stylish combinations of lavish,
expertly-blended ingredients
have rightly earned their
place on the modern cocktail
menu, but pared-back drinks
that offer clean flavours are a
lighter alternative. Just take a
handful of ingredients, some
good-quality rum and blend
for understated perfection. Try
the famous Cuba Libre, as well
as gems like Rum 'n' Currant,
Lounge Lizard and Fox Trot.

PEACH DREAMER

SERVES 1

INGREDIENTS

1 measure white rum

1 measure peach schnapps

3 measures fresh orange juice

crushed ice

1 measure grenadine

1. Shake the white rum, peach schnapps and orange juice well over ice. Strain into a chilled cocktail glass filled with ice.

2. Slowly pour a little grenadine into the glass. Serve immediately.

OLD SOAK

SERVES 1
INGREDIENTS

2 measures golden rum

1 measure
Southern Comfort

1 measure ginger syrup

cracked ice

soda water

1. Shake the golden rum, Southern Comfort and ginger syrup over cracked ice until well frosted.

2. Pour into a chilled cocktail glass filled with ice. Top up with soda water to taste. Serve immediately.

CUBA LIBRE

SERVES 1

INGREDIENTS

cracked ice

2 measures white rum

cola

lime wedge, to decorate

1. Half-fill a chilled cocktail glass with cracked ice.

2. Pour over the rum and top up with cola.

3. Stir gently to mix and decorate with a lime wedge. Serve immediately.

FOX TROT

SERVES 1
INGREDIENTS

juice of ½ lemon or 1 lime

2 dashes orange curaçao

2 measures white rum

cracked ice

orange slice, to decorate

1. Shake the lemon juice, orange curaçao and white rum over cracked ice until well frosted.

2. Strain into a chilled cocktail glass filled with ice. Decorate with an orange slice. Serve immediately.

NELSON'S BLOOD

Admiral Nelson was a hugely prominent figure in the British navy. During his highly decorated career (1771-1805) he secured numerous victories and forged a lasting legacy. However, it was his death in the Battle of Trafalgar, off the coast of Spain, where the origins of the grisly tale of 'Nelson's Blood' can be found.

Nelson died when he took a bullet through the chest from a French sniper. A sea burial was not fitting for a man of Nelson's stature so legend has it that the decision was taken to preserve his body in a barrel of navy rum and return him to Britain. It's said that the barrel was tapped by so many of the crew that when it was eventually opened, only the pickled admiral remained. The term 'Nelson's Blood' as a moniker for rum was adopted almost immediately by the navy and has even been embraced by a handful of brands, pubs and bars around the world.

The true story however is actually quite different. He was in fact preserved in a wine-based spirit (most likely brandy) and he was respectfully guarded day and night. Upon returning to England, coroners supposedly commented on the remarkable preservation of his body. The moral of this tale, never to let the truth get in the way of a good story!

PARISIAN BLONDE

SERVES 1

INGREDIENTS

1 measure dark rum

1 measure orange
curaçao

1 measure cream

cracked ice

orange slice, to decorate

1. Shake the dark rum, orange curaçao and cream over cracked ice until well frosted.

2. Strain into a chilled cocktail glass filled with ice. Decorate with an orange slice. Serve immediately.

ANKLE BREAKER

SERVES 1

INGREDIENTS

2 measures dark rum

1 measure cherry brandy

1 measure lime juice

1 tsp sugar syrup

cracked ice

1. Shake the rum, cherry brandy, lime juice and sugar syrup over cracked ice until well frosted.

2. Strain into a chilled cocktail glass. Serve immediately.

LOUNGE LIZARD

SERVES 1
INGREDIENTS

2 measures dark rum

1 measure amaretto

cracked ice

cola

1. Shake the rum and amaretto over cracked ice until well frosted. Strain into a chilled cocktail glass.

2. Top up with cola and stir gently. Serve immediately.

CIDER BREEZE

SERVES 1
INGREDIENTS

1 measure coconut rum

ice cubes

sparkling cider

apple slice, to decorate

1. Add the rum to a chilled cocktail glass that is half-filled with ice cubes.

2. Top up with the cider. Decorate with an apple slice. Serve immediately.

PALM BEACH

SERVES 1

INGREDIENTS

1 measure white rum

1 measure gin

1 measure pineapple juice

cracked ice

pineapple, to decorate

1. Shake the rum, gin and pineapple juice over cracked ice until well frosted.

2. Strain into a chilled cocktail glass filled with ice. Decorate with pineapple. Serve immediately.

PLANTER'S COCKTAIL

SERVES 1
INGREDIENTS

1 measure rum

juice of ½ lime

1 tsp sugar syrup

dash Angostura bitters

fruit slices, to decorate

1. Shake the rum, lime juice, sugar syrup and Angostura bitters together.

2. Pour into a chilled cocktail glass and decorate with fruit slices. Serve immediately.

OCEAN BREEZE

SERVES 1

INGREDIENTS

1 measure white rum

1 measure amaretto

½ measure blue curaçao

½ measure pineapple juice

cracked ice

soda water

1. Shake the white rum, amaretto, blue curaçao and pineapple juice over cracked ice until well frosted. Strain into a chilled cocktail glass.

2. Top up with soda water. Serve immediately.

RUM 'N' CURRANT

SERVES 1

INGREDIENTS

1 measure dark rum

½ measure blackcurrant cordial

cracked ice

lemonade

1. Shake the rum and blackcurrant cordial over cracked ice until well frosted. Strain into a chilled cocktail glass.

2. Top up with lemonade. Serve immediately.

SPACE ODYSSEY

SERVES 1

INGREDIENTS

1 measure golden rum

2 dashes Angostura bitters

cracked ice

coloured cherries

ginger beer

1. Mix the rum and bitters in a chilled cocktail glass filled with ice and coloured cherries.

2. Top up with ginger beer. Serve immediately.

TAMARA'S TIPPLE

SERVES 1

INGREDIENTS

2 measures dark rum

1 measure crème de cacao

cracked ice

cola

lemon slices

1. Shake the rum and crème de cacao over cracked ice until well frosted. Strain into a chilled cocktail glass filled with ice.

2. Top up with cola and decorate with slices of lemon. Serve immediately.

THE DEVIL

SERVES 1

INGREDIENTS

1 measure dark rum

½ measure red vermouth

cracked ice

black olive, to decorate

1. Shake the rum and vermouth over cracked ice until well frosted. Strain into a chilled cocktail glass filled with ice.

2. Decorate with a black olive. Serve immediately.

CHAPTER 3

INGENIOUS MIXES

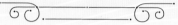

With the increased popularity in rum cocktails, mixologists across the globe have been challenged to create the next big thing: to take classic ingredients and fuse them with unexpected flavours – and the results are as exciting as they are delicious. Here you'll find the Beer & Rum Flip, Salted Caramel Rum Hot Chocolate, Winter Daiquiri and Mermaid Water. Surprising, intriguing and out of the ordinary, these cocktails won't disappoint.

RUM COBBLER

SERVES 1

INGREDIENTS

100 g/3½ oz whisky-barrel woodchips

350 ml/12 fl oz brown rum

crushed ice

splash grenadine

½ measure maraschino liqueur

maraschino cherry, orange slices and lime slices, to decorate

1. This cocktail takes 2 weeks to infuse and you will need a blowtorch. Lay the whisky-barrel chips on a metal tray and place on a heatproof surface.

2. Using a blowtorch, scorch all over the woodchips until about half have blackened. Put the scorched woodchips into a sterilized, sealable jar, then pour in the rum. Keep the rum bottle for later use. Mix and seal the jar. Leave in a cool place for 2 weeks.

3. After 2 weeks, strain the rum through a fine sieve. Fill a lowball glass with ice. Pour in 2 measures of the rum. The rest can be stored for up to 2 months.

4. Add the grenadine and maraschino and stir. Decorate with the cherry, orange and lime. Serve immediately.

WINTER DAIQUIRI

SERVES 1

INGREDIENTS

2 measures golden rum

2 tsp runny honey

2 strips orange zest

2.5-cm/1-inch piece cinnamon stick, halved

1 thin slice fresh ginger

1 allspice berry, crushed

2 tsp fresh orange juice

2 tsp fresh lime juice

cracked ice

1 tsp water

1 tsp caster sugar

large pinch ground cinnamon

1. Add the rum, honey, orange strips, cinnamon, ginger and allspice to a small saucepan and warm gently together for a minute or two. Take off the heat and leave to cool for at least 1 hour, or longer if you have time, so that the flavours can infuse together.

2. When ready to serve, strain the infused rum into a cocktail shaker, reserving the aromatics. Add the orange and lime juice, cracked ice and shake together gently until well frosted.

3. To frost the glass, add the water to a saucer. Add the sugar and ground cinnamon to a second saucer. Dip the rim of a cocktail glass first in the water, then in the sugar. Cut some of the reserved orange into thin strips and add to the glass with a long thin sliver of the reserved cinnamon. Strain the Daiquiri into the glass. Serve immediately.

BLACKBERRY & MINT MOJITO

SERVES 1

INGREDIENTS

1 tbsp fresh lime juice

2 measures white rum

2 measures blackberry mint syrup (see below)

cracked ice

fresh mint sprig

75–125 ml/2½–4 fl oz chilled soda water, to serve

BLACKBERRY MINT SYRUP

10 large fresh mint leaves

115 g/4 oz blackberries

55 g/2 oz caster sugar

1. To make the blackberry mint syrup, rub the mint leaves in your hands to release their flavour then add to the base of a small saucepan. Sprinkle in the blackberries then add the sugar and two measures of water. Heat gently, stirring occasionally until the sugar has dissolved, then boil for 1 minute. Take off the heat and leave to cool for 30 minutes.

2. Press the blackberry mixture through a fine sieve to remove the blackberry seeds. Pour into a sterilized, sealable jar and chill in the refrigerator.

3. To make the cocktail, add the lime juice, rum and blackberry mint syrup to a cocktail shaker with a handful of cracked ice. The rest of the blackberry mint syrup can be stored in the refrigerator for up to 3 days. Shake vigorously until well frosted. Pour into a chilled cocktail glass filled with ice and a sprig of mint. Top up with chilled soda water to taste. Serve immediately.

CRANBERRY MULES

SERVES 1

INGREDIENTS

2 tbsp cranberry syrup
(see below)

2 measures white rum

4 measures ginger beer

cracked ice

frozen cranberries,
to decorate

CRANBERRY SYRUP

115 g/4 oz frozen
cranberries

115 g/4 oz caster sugar

225 ml/8 fl oz water

1. First make the cranberry syrup by adding the cranberries, sugar and water to a small saucepan. Cook over a gentle heat, stirring occasionally until the sugar has completely dissolved then increase the heat slightly and simmer for about 5 minutes or until the cranberries have burst and the liquid is thick and syrupy. Cover and leave to cool.

2. Purée if liked, then pour into a sterilized, sealable jar and chill in the refrigerator.

3. To make the cocktail, add 2 tablespoons of the cranberry syrup to a glass filled with ice. The rest of the syrup can be stored in the refrigerator for up to 3 days.

4. Add the white rum and ginger beer to a cocktail shaker with some cracked ice. Shake together until well frosted and frothy. Pour into the glass to create a two-tone effect. Finish with a few frozen cranberries. Serve immediately.

THE DAILY RATION

No drink has stronger ties with the navy than rum. The first official rum rations for British sailors began in 1655 and continued up until 1970.

Fresh water never travelled well on ships and beer would often sour, becoming a putrid barrel of rancid, stagnant filth, especially when traveling in warmer parts of the world. Rum however, thanks to its high alcoholic strength, would travel indefinitely. Aside from its preserving qualities it served another important role – keeping up morale and offering much needed respite from what would have been for many a hard and uncertain life at sea.

The quantities of the rum ration varied over the centuries as fairly legitimate concerns were raised over the competency of intoxicated crews, bearing in mind the ration was likely consumed on top of more private stashes of rum. Admiral Edward Vernon was responsible for a major change in the ration when he insisted that the half pint ration of rum be watered down and flavoured with lime in order to ward off drunkenness. The quantity of rum didn't change, so the new drink was not badly received by the crew. Plus the lime helped ward off scurvy, potentially helping to save lives.

The drink soon became known as 'grog', taking its name from Vernon's nickname 'Old Grogman' – a name that he acquired through routinely wearing a weatherproof jacket known then as a 'Grogman'. Admiral Vernon, 'Old Grogman', could arguably be credited for creating one of the very first rum cocktails.

MANDARIN & LIME GINGER BEER

SERVES 1

INGREDIENTS

1 lime

½ mandarin

2 measures dark rum

ice cubes

150 ml/5 fl oz ginger beer

lime wedges, to decorate

1. Cut the lime and mandarin into wedges.

2. Place the lime and mandarin into a cocktail shaker. Use a muddler for about 10 seconds to crush the fruit and to release its oils.

3. Add the rum and stir with a bar spoon.

4. Pour the rum mixture into a Collins or highball glass.

5. Add a few ice cubes and top up with the ginger beer.

6. Decorate with lime wedges. Serve immediately.

POLAR BEAR

SERVES 1

INGREDIENTS

2 measures light rum

2 measures advocaat

juice of 1 passion fruit, strained, seeds reserved to decorate

crushed ice

lemonade

1. Blend the rum, advocaat and most of the passion fruit juice with ice in a blender for about 10 seconds until thick and frothy.

2. Strain into a chilled cocktail glass filled with ice and top up with lemonade to taste.

3. Finally, swirl the remaining passion fruit juice, with the reserved seeds on top of the ice. Serve immediately.

CHAMBORD SOUR

SERVES 1

INGREDIENTS

ice cubes

1 measure Chambord

1 measure rum

1 measure lemon juice

½ egg white

1 tbsp sugar syrup

blackberry, to decorate

1. Chill a coupe or coupette glass.

2. Put the ice cubes into a cocktail shaker. Pour the liquid ingredients over the ice cubes.

3. Shake the cocktail shaker vigorously until the mixture creates foam. Strain into a chilled cocktail glass.

4. Decorate the cocktail with the blackberry. Serve immediately.

MERMAID WATER

SERVES 1
INGREDIENTS

2 measures spiced rum

1 measure coconut rum

1 tbsp fresh lime juice

175 ml/6 fl oz pineapple juice

ice cubes

fresh lime and lemon slices

2 tsp blue curaçao

small pineapple pieces, peel left on, to decorate

1. Add the spiced rum, coconut rum and lime juice to a cocktail shaker then pour in the pineapple juice and add a handful of ice cubes. Shake vigorously together until well frosted.

2. Pour the rum mixture and ice into a tall glass and add lime and lemon slices. Drizzle the blue caraçao over the top.

3. Thread the pineapple pieces on to a cocktail stick and arrange on the top of the glass. Serve immediately.

BEER & RUM FLIP

SERVES 4

INGREDIENTS

300 ml/10 fl oz stout

2 measures dark rum

2 measures maple syrup

2 eggs

½ tsp nutmeg, to decorate

1. Gently heat the stout in a medium saucepan over a medium heat.

2. Pour the rum and maple syrup into a blender. Crack in the eggs.

3. When the stout has almost come to the boil, pour it carefully into the blender and blend for 30 seconds, or until the contents are nice and frothy.

4. Divide the flip between four snifter glasses and decorate each drink with a little nutmeg. Serve immediately.

GOLD COFFEE

SERVES 1

INGREDIENTS

1 measure dark rum

1 measure curaçao

3 measures strong cold
black coffee

ice cubes

1 scoop vanilla ice cream

2 tsp strained
passion fruit sauce

1. Put the dark rum, curaçao and coffee into a blender. Add some ice cubes and blend until slushy.

2. Pour into a chilled glass, add the ice cream, and spoon over the passion fruit sauce. Serve immediately.

HONEY, PEACH & AGAVE INFUSION

SERVES 1

INGREDIENTS

2 ripe peaches, cut into wedges

10 peppercorns

2 star anise

½ vanilla pod, split

1 cinnamon stick

2 tbsp agave syrup

2 tbsp honey

350 ml/12 fl oz tequila

ice cubes

1 measure rum

1 measure lime juice

1 egg white

1 measure triple sec

peach slice, to decorate

1. This cocktail takes 1 month to infuse. Place the peach wedges in a sterilized, sealable jar. Add the peppercorns, star anise, vanilla, cinnamon, agave, honey and tequila. Keep the tequila bottle for later use.

2. Mix and seal. Leave in a cool place for 1 month. After 1 month, strain the tequila through a fine sieve. Once strained, pour the tequila back into its bottle. Place 1 measure of the tequila into an ice-filled cocktail shaker. The rest of the tequila can be stored for up to 2 months. Add the rum, lime juice, egg white and triple sec.

3. Shake vigorously until well frosted. Strain into an ice-filled lowball glass and decorate with the peach slice. Serve immediately.

NIRVANA

SERVES 1

INGREDIENTS

2 measures dark rum

½ measure grenadine

½ measure tamarind syrup

1 tsp sugar syrup

cracked ice

grapefruit juice

1. Shake the rum, grenadine, tamarind syrup and sugar syrup over ice until well frosted.

2. Strain into a chilled cocktail glass filled with ice.

3. Top up with grapefruit juice. Serve immediately.

POLYNESIAN SOUR

SERVES 1

INGREDIENTS

crushed ice

2 measures light rum

½ measure guava juice

½ measure lemon juice

½ measure orange juice

1. Put the crushed ice cubes, light rum, guava juice, lemon juice and orange juice into a blender and blend until smooth.

2. Strain into a chilled cocktail glass filled with ice cubes. Serve immediately.

SALTED CARAMEL RUM HOT CHOCOLATE

SERVES 4

INGREDIENTS

2 tbsp granulated sugar

1 tbsp water

salt flakes

200 ml/7 fl oz milk

40 g/1½ oz dark chocolate, broken into pieces

1 tsp cocoa powder

pinch ground cinnamon

1 measure dark rum

shaved or grated dark chocolate, to decorate

mini marshmallows, to serve (optional)

1. Add the sugar and water to a small heavy-based saucepan and heat gently, without stirring until the sugar has completely dissolved.

2. Bring to the boil and boil rapidly for 4–5 minutes, again without stirring until the sugar syrup begins to turn golden around the edges. Keep a very close eye on it at this stage and continue to heat until the syrup is a rich golden brown all over.

3. Take the pan off the heat, add the salt, swirl to mix then gradually pour in the milk. Stand well back as you add the milk as the syrup can spit. Put the pan back over a low heat and stir to mix the caramel and milk together. Add the chocolate. Stir the cocoa powder with a little water to make a paste and add it with the cinnamon. Keep stirring until smooth.

4. When the chocolate mix is hot but not boiling, stir in the rum, warm together then pour into four heatproof glass mugs. Sprinkle with shaved or grated chocolate. Add mini marshmallows, if liked.

ZOMBIE

SERVES 1

INGREDIENTS

2 measures dark rum

2 measures white rum

1 measure golden rum

1 measure triple sec

1 measure lime juice

1 measure orange juice

1 measure pineapple juice

1 measure guava juice

1 tbsp grenadine

1 tbsp orgeat syrup

1 tsp Pernod

crushed ice

fresh mint sprig and
pineapple wedge,
to decorate

1. Shake the liquid ingredients over ice until well frosted.

2. Strain into a chilled cocktail glass.

3. Decorate with the fresh mint and the pineapple wedge. Serve immediately.

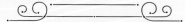

CHAPTER 4

MYSTERIOUS BLENDS

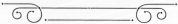

The mystery of a good thriller is often alluded to in the name – a dash of imminent danger, an air of the supernatural or a good dose of suspense. The recipes in this chapter certainly conjure up this sense of intrigue and peril in their ambiguous names and dramatic appearance. Here you'll find the Black Widow, White Lion, Green Devil and Dragon Lady – proceed with caution...

FLAMING MAI TAI

SERVES 1

INGREDIENTS

1 measure dark rum

½ measure triple sec

½ measure brandy

125 ml/4 fl oz pineapple juice

½ measure almond syrup

ice cubes

55 g/2 oz chopped fresh pineapple

½ tsp cinnamon

½ measure 151 overproof rum

mint leaves, to decorate

1. Shake the rum, triple sec, brandy, pineapple juice and almond syrup over ice until well frosted.

2. Strain the cocktail into a heatproof hurricane glass filled with ice cubes.

3. Place the chopped pineapple, cinnamon and 151 rum into a mixing glass. Stir with a bar spoon to combine.

4. Tilt the mixing glass and light the rum mixture with a long match. With care and using flame-resistant gloves, pour the lit rum mixture into the cocktail in the hurricane glass.

5. Allow the flames to die down and the drink to cool completely before drinking. Decorate with mint leaves. Serve immediately.

BLACK WIDOW

SERVES 1

INGREDIENTS

²/₃ measure dark rum

¹/₃ measure Southern Comfort

juice ½ lime

dash curaçao

cracked ice

soda water

lime slices, to decorate

1. Shake the rum, Southern Comfort, lime juice and curaçao well together over ice and strain into a chilled tumbler filled with ice.

2. Top up with soda water and decorate with lime slices. Serve immediately.

MYSTERIOUS

SERVES 1

INGREDIENTS

1 measure dark rum

1 measure orange
curaçao

½ measure coffee liqueur

½ measure fresh
orange juice

ice cubes

1 tbsp double cream,
to decorate

1. Shake dark rum, orange curaçao, coffee liqueur and orange juice over ice until well frosted.

2. Strain into a chilled cocktail glass and top with cream. Serve immediately.

RUM AND PIRACY

Ask someone to draw a pirate and you will almost certainly get all the classic features: the eye patch, peg leg, parrot on the shoulder and, of course, a bottle of rum. The pirate stereotype has evolved over the decades, shaped through modern cinema and popular culture. But at least one part of the stereotype is pretty accurate – the rum.

In reality, pirates existed in a culture far removed from the stylized Hollywood interpretations. As social outcasts, and men living on the edge, they would be happy drinking anything they could get their hands on. It just so happened that the majority of ships moving around the trade triangle between the Americas, Europe and Africa would have been carrying rum, a universal currency of the time, so it was easy pickings.

However, some experts would argue that pirates were actually more fond of brandy. This isn't that surprising as, for large chapters of history, pirates were licensed to attack Spanish ships to help the British navy. These ships heading from Spain to the colonies would have likely been carrying high quality grape-based spirits. Whatever pirates were drinking, it's unquestionable that booze was at the heart of many pirate ships!

GREEN DEVIL

SERVES 1

INGREDIENTS

lime juice

icing sugar

1 measure light rum

½ measure blue curaçao

1 measure orange juice

cracked ice

lime slice, to decorate

1. Dip the rim of a large cocktail glass into lime juice and then into sugar to create sugar frosting.

2. Set aside to dry. Shake the light rum, blue curaçao and orange juice over ice until well frosted.

3. Pour into the frosted glass and decorate with a slice of lime. Serve immediately.

EYE-OPENER

SERVES 1
INGREDIENTS

1 measure rum

2 dashes crème de noyaux

2 dashes absinthe

2 dashes curaçao

1 egg yolk

1 tsp icing sugar

cracked ice

1. Shake the rum, crème de noyaux, absinthe, curaçao, egg yolk and icing sugar over ice until well frosted.

2. Strain into a chilled cocktail glass. Serve immediately.

TONGUE TWISTER

SERVES 1

INGREDIENTS

1 measure light rum

½ measure coconut
cream liqueur

½ measure
orange curaçao

1 measure lemon juice

cracked ice

grated nutmeg,
to decorate

1. Shake the light rum, coconut cream liqueur, orange curaçao and lemon juice over ice until well frosted.

2. Strain into a chilled cocktail glass filled with ice and sprinkle with grated nutmeg. Serve immediately.

WHITE LION

SERVES 1

INGREDIENTS

dash Angostura bitters

dash grenadine

2 measures white rum

1 measure lemon juice

1 tsp sugar syrup

cracked ice

1. Shake the Angostura bitters, grenadine, white rum, lemon juice and sugar syrup over ice until well frosted.

2. Strain into a chilled cocktail glass. Serve immediately.

TIGER'S MILK

SERVES 1

INGREDIENTS

2 measures golden rum

1½ measures brandy

1 tsp sugar syrup

125 ml/4 fl oz milk

crushed ice

ground cinnamon and
a cinnamon stick,
to decorate

1. Put the rum, brandy, sugar syrup and milk into a blender with crushed ice and blend until well combined.

2. Pour into a chilled cocktail glass. Sprinkle with ground cinnamon and decorate with a cinnamon stick. Serve immediately.

ZOMBIE PRINCE

SERVES 1

INGREDIENTS

dash Angostura bitters

1 measure white rum

1 measure golden rum

1 measure dark rum

½ measure lemon juice

½ measure orange juice

½ measure grapefruit juice

cracked ice

1 tsp brown sugar

1. Shake the Angostura bitters, white rum, golden rum, dark rum, lemon juice, orange juice and grapefruit juice over ice until well frosted. Then add the sugar.

2. Stir to mix well, then strain into a tall chilled cocktail glass filled with ice. Serve immediately.

RAIL-ROADSTER

SERVES 1

INGREDIENTS

1 tsp fine zest of lime

1 tsp icing sugar

1½ measures white rum

½ measure Galliano

1 measure lime juice

cracked ice

dry ginger ale

1. Mix the lime zest and sugar together.

2. Rub the rim of a glass with a little rum, then dip it into the sugar to coat thoroughly. Set aside to dry.

3. Shake the white rum, Galliano and lime juice over the cracked ice until well frosted.

4. Pour into the cocktail glass filled with ice and top up with a little ginger ale. Serve immediately.

MYSTERIOUS BLENDS

FIREMAN'S SOUR

SERVES 1

INGREDIENTS

2 measures white rum

1½ measures lime juice

1 tbsp grenadine

1 tsp sugar syrup

cracked ice

cocktail cherry, to decorate

1. Shake the white rum, lime juice, grenadine and sugar syrup over ice until well frosted.

2. Strain into a chilled cocktail glass and decorate with a cocktail cherry. Serve immediately.

BIG CITY MIST

SERVES 1
INGREDIENTS

1 measure Irish Mist

1 measure dark rum

2 measures passion fruit juice

1 measure pink grapefruit juice

dash grenadine

cracked ice

1. Shake Irish Mist, dark rum, passion fruit juce, pink grapefruit juice and grenadine over ice until well frosted.

2. Pour into a chilled cocktail glass filled with ice. Serve immediately.

DRAGON LADY

SERVES 1

INGREDIENTS

1 measure golden rum

1 measure orange juice

dash white curaçao

dash grenadine

cracked ice

bitter lemon, chilled

orange slice, to decorate

1. Stir golden run, orange juice, white curaçao and grenadine over ice until well frosted.

2. Strain into a highball glass filled with ice and top up with bitter lemon.

3. Decorate with a slice of orange. Serve immediately.

XYZ

SERVES 1

INGREDIENTS

½ measure fresh
lemon juice

½ measure white rum

½ measure Cointreau

cracked ice

lime slice, to decorate

1. Shake the lemon juice, white rum and Cointreau over ice until well frosted.

2. Strain into a chilled cocktail glass filled with ice and decorate with a slice of lime. Serve immediately.

BEAUTIFUL DREAMER

SERVES 1

INGREDIENTS

2 measures white rum

1 measure coconut cream,
beaten until creamy

1 measure guava juice

1 measure pineapple juice

cracked ice

melon or guava slices,
to decorate

1. Shake white rum, coconut cream, guava juice and pineapple juice over ice until well frosted.

2. Pour into a cocktail glass filled with ice and decorate with fruit slices. Serve immediately.

CHAPTER 5

ISLAND PARADISE

Transport yourself to total island paradise with the recipes in this chapter. Think sunshine, palm trees and waves of turquoise water washing onto golden sand as you prepare fresh fruit and sunny mixers. Here you'll find recipes like Tropical Sangria, Blue Hawaiian, Barbados Sunset and Strawberry Colada that all conjure up idyllic holiday vibes with just a simple twist of the cocktail shaker.

PEACH DAIQUIRI

SERVES 1
INGREDIENTS

2 measures white rum

1 measure lime juice

½ tsp sugar syrup

½ peach, peeled, stoned and chopped

ice cubes

1. Put the white rum, lime juice, sugar syrup and peach in a blender and blend until smooth.

2. Pour, without straining, into a chilled cocktail glass filled with ice. Serve immediately.

STRAWBERRY COLADA

SERVES 1

INGREDIENTS

3 measures golden rum

4 measures pineapple juice

1 measure coconut cream

cracked ice

6 strawberries

pineapple wedge and halved strawberry, to decorate

1. Put the rum, pineapple juice, coconut cream and ice into a blender.

2. Add the strawberries to the blender. Blend until smooth.

3. Pour, without straining, into a chilled cocktail glass. Decorate with a pineapple wedge and strawberry half. Serve immediately.

TROPICAL FRUIT PUNCH

SERVES 6

INGREDIENTS

1 small ripe mango

4 tbsp lime juice

1 tsp finely grated
fresh ginger

1 tbsp light brown sugar

1.2 litres/2 pints
orange juice

1.2 litres/2 pints
pineapple juice

90 ml/3 fl oz white rum

crushed ice

fruit slices, to decorate

1. Put the mango, lime juice, ginger and sugar into a blender and blend until smooth.

2. Add the orange juice, pineapple juice and the rum and blend again for a few seconds until smooth.

3. Divide the crushed ice between six chilled cocktail glasses and pour the punch over. Decorate with fruit slices Serve immediately.

TROPICAL SANGRIA

SERVES 1

INGREDIENTS

85 g/3 oz prepared watermelon, diced

55 g/2 oz prepared pineapple, diced

¼ small papaya, deseeded, peeled and diced

½ lime, cut into wedges

2 measures golden rum

125 ml/4 fl oz Spanish white Rioja wine

90 ml/3 fl oz pineapple juice

75–125 ml/2½–4 fl oz chilled soda water or sparkling mineral water, to serve

ice cubes

1. Add the diced watermelon, pineapple and papaya to a mason jar. Squeeze the juice from the lime over the top and add the squeezed wedges to the jar.

2. Pour over the rum, white wine and pineapple juice and stir together. Screw on the lid then chill in the refrigerator for 30 minutes, or longer if you have time, so that the flavours can infuse together.

3. When ready to serve, pour the soda water into the jar, stir together then add ice. Serve immediately.

BAJAN SUN

SERVES 1

INGREDIENTS

1 measure white rum

1 measure mandarin brandy

1 measure orange juice

1 measure pineapple juice

cracked ice

splash grenadine

fresh pineapple slice and cocktail cherry, to decorate

1. Shake the rum, brandy, orange juice and pineapple juice over cracked ice until well frosted.

2. Add the grenadine and shake vigorously.

3. Strain into a chilled cocktail glass and decorate with a pineapple slice and cocktail cherry. Serve immediately.

BLUE HAWAIIAN

SERVES 1

INGREDIENTS

2 measures white rum

½ measure blue curaçao

1 measure pineapple juice

½ measure coconut cream

cracked ice

pineapple wedge,
to decorate

1. Shake the rum, blue curaçao, pineapple juice and coconut cream over cracked ice until well frosted. Strain into a chilled cocktail glass.

2. Decorate with the pineapple wedge. Serve immediately.

BANANA COLADA

INGREDIENTS

2 measures white rum

4 measures pineapple juice

1 measure Malibu

1 banana, peeled and sliced

crushed ice

pineapple wedges, to decorate

1. Put the white rum, pineapple juice, Malibu, sliced banana and ice in a blender and blend until smooth.

2. Pour, without straining, into a chilled cocktail glass. Decorate with pineapple wedges. Serve immediately.

CUBAN SPECIAL

SERVES 1

INGREDIENTS

2 measures white rum

1 measure lime juice

1 tbsp pineapple juice

1 tsp triple sec

cracked ice

pineapple wedges,
to decorate

1. Shake the rum, lime juice, pineapple juice and triple sec over cracked ice until well frosted. Strain into a chilled cocktail glass.

2. Decorate with pineapple wedges. Serve immediately.

COCO ROCO

SERVES 1

INGREDIENTS

2 measures fresh
coconut juice

½ measure white rum

½ measure apricot brandy

½ measure coconut milk

cracked ice

1. Put the fresh coconut juice, white rum, apricot brandy, coconut milk and cracked ice into a blender and blend until smooth.

2. Pour into a chilled cocktail glass filled with ice. Serve immediately.

RUM AND REVOLUTION

Throughout the 18th century the Americas prospered on the back of the lucrative crops cultivated by slave labour. The trade in molasses to make rum was widespread and distilleries making rum were cropping up all over the North East region of the US, known as New England.

Ships loaded with molasses were making their way from the French West Indies to the rum distillers of New England, and the profits were tidy. A gallon of French molasses was typically sold for 1 shilling – once fermented and distilled into rum, it was selling for 6 shillings a gallon. Numerous New England distilleries and French colonies were profiting at the expense of the British Crown. The French molasses was leaving such a bad taste in the mouths of the British government that it made efforts to stop the illicit ships heading north. Naval efforts had failed so the British responded with hefty taxes on the New Englanders, taxes which encouraged smuggling and corruption amongst the colonial officials. This encouraged the idea of independence.

One champion of American independence, a young George Washington, was running for election in the Virginia House of Burgesses in 1757. Records suggest he served up 28 gallons of neat rum along with 50 gallons of rum punch and lashings of wine and beer to locals during his campaign. His crowd-pleasing efforts led to a landslide victory. After independence and his presidency was achieved, George went on to set up his own distillery.

CALYPSO STING

SERVES 1

INGREDIENTS

1 measure dark rum

1 measure Malibu

½ measure orange curaçao

½ measure orange juice

dash fresh lime juice

cracked ice

tonic water

dash Angostura bitters

cherry and a slice of lime, to decorate

1. Shake the dark rum, Malibu, orange curaçao, orange juice and lime juice over cracked ice until well frosted. Strain into a chilled cocktail glass filled with ice and top up with tonic water.

2. Finish with a drop or two of Angostura bitters, and dress with a cherry and a lime slice. Serve immediately.

BARBADOS SUNSET

SERVES 1
INGREDIENTS

1½ measures golden rum

1 measure coconut rum

2 measures orange juice

2 measures pineapple juice

dash strawberry syrup

cracked ice

fruit slices, to decorate

1. Shake the golden rum, coconut rum, orange juice, pineapple juice and strawberry syrup over cracked ice until well frosted. Strain into a chilled cocktail glass.

2. Add more ice and decorate with slices of fruit. Serve immediately.

AMIGOS PIÑA COLADA

SERVES 4
INGREDIENTS

125 ml/4 fl oz white rum

225 ml/8 fl oz pineapple juice

5 measures coconut cream

2 measures dark rum

2 measures single cream

crushed ice

pineapple wedges, to decorate

1. Put the white rum, pineapple juice, coconut cream, dark rum, cream and ice into a blender and blend until smooth.

2. Pour, without straining, into chilled cocktail glasses and decorate with pineapple wedges. Serve immediately.

BANANA DAIQUIRI

SERVES 1
INGREDIENTS

2 measures white rum, chilled

½ measure triple sec, chilled

½ measure lime juice

½ measure single cream, chilled

1 tsp sugar syrup

¼ banana, peeled and sliced

lime slice, to decorate

1. Put white rum, triple sec, lime juice, single cream and sugar syrup into a blender and blend.

2. Add the banana and blend until smooth.

3. Pour, without straining, into a chilled cocktail glass.

4. Decorate with a lime slice. Serve immediately.

POLYNESIA

SERVES 1

INGREDIENTS

2 measures white rum

2 measures passion fruit juice

1 measure lime juice

1 egg white

cracked ice

dash Angostura bitters

1. Shake the rum, passion fruit juice, lime juice and egg white over cracked ice with a dash of Angostura bitters until well frosted.

2. Strain into a chilled cocktail glass. Serve immediately.

PINEAPPLE PLANTER'S PUNCH

SERVES 1

INGREDIENTS

1 measure white rum

1 measure pineapple juice

juice of ½ lime

½ measure white curaçao

dash maraschino

cracked ice

kiwi and pineapple slice, to decorate

1. Shake the white rum, pineapple juice, lime juice, white curaçao and maraschino over cracked ice until well frosted. Strain into a chilled cocktail glass.

2. Decorate with the fruit slices. Serve immediately.

SAILOR'S RUM PUNCH

SERVES 1

INGREDIENTS

1 measure lemon juice

2 measures sugar syrup

3 measures strong rum

few shakes of
Angostura bitters

4 measures fruit juice

cracked ice

fruit pieces, to decorate

1. Shake the lemon juice, sugar syrup, rum and Angostura bitters over cracked ice until well frosted. Set aside to let the flavours develop.

2. To serve, stir in the fruit juice and pour into a chilled cocktail glass with a little more ice. Decorate with fruit pieces and serve immediately.

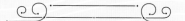

CHAPTER 6

CREATIVE COOLERS

Warmer weather calls for an ice-cold cooler and the recipes in this chapter provide a creative selection of perfectly chilled drinks. Think easy-breezy combined with a touch of ingenuity here. Frozen cocktails like Frozen Daiquiri and Palm Breeze provide instant icy satisfaction, while Piña Colada Pops and Mojito Pops combine classic cocktails with the novelty of a strictly adults-only ice pop.

MANGO FREEZE

SERVES 4

INGREDIENTS

6 measures golden rum

4 measures mango juice

4 measures fresh
orange juice

1 measure sugar syrup

good squeeze lemon juice

1 egg white

cracked ice

lemonade

mango slices, to decorate

1. Put the golden rum, mango juice, orange juice, sugar syrup, lemon juice and egg white in a blender and blend with ice until frothy and frozen.

2. Pour into frozen cocktail glasses and top up with lemonade. Decorate with a slice of mango and serve immediately.

FROZEN DAIQUIRI

SERVES 1
INGREDIENTS

2 measures white rum

1 measure lime juice

1 tsp sugar syrup

crushed ice

lime slice, to decorate

1. Put the rum, lime juice and sugar syrup in a blender with ice and blend until slushy and frozen.

2. Pour into a chilled cocktail glass and decorate with a lime slice. Serve immediately.

JAMAICAN COOLER

SERVES 1

INGREDIENTS

1½ measures Jamaican rum

ice cubes

soda water

lemon slices, to decorate

1. Pour the rum into a chilled cocktail glass filled with ice.

2. Top up with soda water and decorate with lemon slices. Serve immediately.

MOJITO POPS

MAKES 8

INGREDIENTS

juice of 6 limes

600 ml/1 pint chilled soda water

50 g/1¾ oz fresh mint leaves

3 limes, cut into wedges

100 g/3½ oz caster sugar

2 tbsp white rum

YOU WILL ALSO NEED

8 x 100ml/3½ fl oz ice pop moulds

8 ice pop sticks

1. Put the lime juice and soda water into a measuring jug and stir together well.

2. Stir in the mint leaves, lime wedges, sugar and rum. Using a 'muddler' or thick wooden spoon or mallet, mash together all the ingredients until well blended.

3. Pour the mixture into 8 x 100 ml/ 3½ fl oz ice pop moulds. Divide the lime wedges and mint leaves evenly between them. Insert the ice pop sticks and freeze for 10–12 hours, or until firm.

4. To unmould the ice pops, dip the frozen moulds into warm water for a few seconds and gently release the pops while holding the sticks.

STRAWBERRIES & CREAM

SERVES 1

INGREDIENTS

1 measure light rum, chilled

1 measure grapefruit juice, chilled

1 measure double cream

5–6 large strawberries, hulled (save one to serve)

cracked ice

1. Put the light rum, grapefruit juice, cream and strawberries in a blender with ice and blend until slushy and frozen.

2. Pour into a chilled cocktail glass and decorate with the remaining strawberry. Serve immediately.

FROZEN STRAWBERRY DAIQUIRI

SERVES 1

INGREDIENTS

2 measures white rum

1 measure lime juice

1 tsp sugar syrup

7 large strawberries, hulled
(save one to serve)

crushed ice

1. Put the white rum, lime juice, sugar syrup and strawberries in a blender with ice and blend until slushy.

2. Pour into a chilled cocktail glass and decorate with the reserved strawberry. Serve immediately.

JOSIAH'S BAY FLOAT

SERVES 1
INGREDIENTS

2 measures golden rum

1 measure Galliano

2 measures pineapple juice

1 measure lime juice

4 tsp sugar syrup

cracked ice

Champagne

pineapple shell, to serve

fruit slices, to decorate

1. Shake the golden rum, Galliano, pineapple juice, lime juice and sugar syrup over cracked ice until well frosted.

2. Strain into the pineapple shell.

3. Top up with Champagne and decorate with fruit slices. Serve immediately.

THE FUTURE OF RUM

The trend for cocktails using carefully selected ingredients and bespoke flavour combinations has pushed classic rum drinks to exciting new creations. With a growing demand for quality spirits and drinks with provenance, new producers and craft distillers are constantly concocting inventive and high-quality rums.

The sugar industry in the West Indies and the old colonies has been declining for decades, but as a result, established rum producers are responding by securing their own plantations and sugar-cane needs, adding more provenance and control over their processes in turn. With controlled and well-cultivated cane fields comes better cane juice and better rums, which is great news for consumers.

With time, the industry is hopeful that more solid and official guidelines surrounding the production of Caribbean rum will emerge. Clear guidelines surrounding the sweetening of rums prior to bottling and ageing in turn allows for greater transparency in the industry, ultimately helping consumers to make informed choices.

So long as the world keeps producing sugar, sugar-cane spirits will always be with us. Innovative brands will keep pushing boundaries for new audiences and armed with clear definitions and a focus on quality they will appeal to the serious spirit enthusiasts of the world.

RUM SWIZZLE

SERVES 1

INGREDIENTS

2 measures dark rum

1 measure fresh lime juice

½ measure sugar syrup

2–3 dashes Angostura bitters

crushed ice

1. Put the dark rum, lime juice, sugar syrup and Angostura bitters in a blender with ice and blend until frothy and part frozen.

2. Pour into an iced tumbler with more ice to taste. Serve immediately.

FROZEN PINEAPPLE DAIQUIRI

SERVES 1

INGREDIENTS

2 measures white rum

1 measure lime juice

½ tsp pineapple syrup

55 g/2 oz finely chopped fresh pineapple

crushed ice

pineapple wedges, to decorate

1. Put the white rum, lime juice, pineapple syrup and chopped pineapple in a blender with ice and blend until slushy.

2. Pour into a chilled cocktail glass. Decorate with pineapple wedges. Serve immediately.

CARIBBEAN BLUES

SERVES 1

INGREDIENTS

1 measure white rum

½ measure blue curaçao

good squeeze lime juice

¼ measure sugar syrup

ice cubes

soda water

3 frozen lime slices,
to decorate

1. Mix the white rum, blue curaçao, lime juice and sugar syrup in chilled cocktail glass with a few ice cubes.

2. Top up with soda water and decorate with frozen slices of lime. Serve immediately.

PLANTER'S PUNCH REFRESHER

SERVES 1

INGREDIENTS

2 measures rum

2 measures lime juice

1–2 tsp grenadine

dash Angostura bitters

cracked ice

soda water

1. Shake the rum, lime juice, grenadine and Angostura bitters over cracked ice until well frosted.

2. Strain into a chilled cocktail glass filled with ice.

3. Top up with soda water. Serve immediately.

BEACH BUM

SERVES 1
INGREDIENTS

1 measure dark rum

1 measure peach brandy

1 measure lime juice

½ mango, stoned, peeled and chopped

cracked ice

lime slice, to decorate

1. Put the dark rum, brandy, lime juice and mango in a blender and blend at a slow speed for about 10 seconds.

2. Pour into a chilled cocktail glass filled with ice and decorate with a slice of lime. Serve immediately.

FROZEN PEACH DAIQUIRI

SERVES 1

INGREDIENTS

½ peach, stoned and chopped

2 measures white rum

1 measure lime juice

1 tsp sugar syrup

cracked ice

peach slice, to decorate

1. Put the peach, white rum, lime juice and sugar syrup into a blender with ice and blend until slushy.

2. Pour into a chilled cocktail glass. Decorate with a peach slice. Serve immediately.

PIÑA COLADA POPS

MAKES 8
INGREDIENTS

600 g/1 lb 5 oz pineapple flesh, finely diced

200 ml/7 fl oz coconut milk

6 tbsp caster sugar

2 tbsp Malibu

YOU WILL ALSO NEED

8 x 100 ml/3½ fl oz ice pop moulds

8 ice pop sticks

1. Drop a tablespoon of the diced pineapple flesh into each of 8 x 100 ml/3½ fl oz ice pop moulds.

2. Put the remaining pineapple flesh in a blender with the coconut milk, sugar and Malibu and whizz until smooth.

3. Sieve using a fine metal sieve, pressing down to extract all the juice. Discard the solids. Pour the mixture into the ice pop moulds. Insert the ice pop sticks and freeze for 6–8 hours, or until firm.

4. To unmould the ice pops, dip the frozen moulds into warm water for a few seconds and gently release the pops while holding the sticks.

CASABLANCA

SERVES 1

INGREDIENTS

3 measures white rum

4 measures pineapple juice

2 measures coconut cream

cracked ice

pineapple wedge, to decorate

1. Shake white rum, pineapple juice and coconut cream over cracked ice until well frosted.

2. Strain into chilled cocktail glasses with ice.

3. Decorate with pineapple. Serve immediately.

PALM BREEZE

SERVES 1

INGREDIENTS

1 measure white rum

1 measure gin

2–3 measures pineapple juice

cracked ice

fresh pineapple slice, to decorate

1. Shake the white rum, gin and pineapple juice over cracked ice until well frosted.

2. Strain into chilled cocktail glasses.

3. Decorate with a slice of fresh pineapple. Serve immediately.

INDEX

This edition published by Parragon Books Ltd
in 2018
LOVE FOOD is an imprint of Parragon Books Ltd

Parragon Books Ltd
Chartist House
15–17 Trim Street
Bath BA1 1HA, UK
www.parragon.co.uk/love-food
www.parragon.com.au/love-food

ISBN 978-1-4748-9726-6

Printed in China

Introduction: Joe Clark
New recipes: Sara Lewis
New photography: Mike Cooper

Notes for the Reader
This book uses both metric and imperial
measurements. Follow the same units of
measurement throughout; do not mix metric
and imperial. All spoon measurements are
level: teaspoons are assumed to be 5 ml, and
tablespoons are assumed to be 15 ml.
One measure is assumed to be 25 ml/¾ fl
oz. Unless otherwise stated, milk is assumed
to be full fat, eggs and individual fruits and
vegetables are medium, pepper is freshly
ground black pepper and salt is table salt. A
pinch of salt is calculated as ¹⁄₁₆ of a teaspoon.

Please consume alcohol responsibly.